Corn

Victoria Blakemore

To Jen, for always sharing your ideas and being there to

listen.

© 2017 Victoria Blakemore

vblakemore.author@gmail.com

Copyright info/picture credits

Table of Contents

What is Corn?

Corn is a cereal crop. It is a member of the grass family. It can also be called **maize**.

Corn is usually yellow. It can also be blue, purple, green, red, or white.

A corn plant can be between three and ten feet tall.

History of Corn

Corn was first grown in Mexico thousands of years ago. It was an important food source.

It spread through North and South America. Europeans came to the Americas and brought corn back to Europe with them.

Corn is now a popular food worldwide. It is grown on every continent except Antarctica.

Corn Stalks

The corn stalk is the stem of the plant. It is hard and keeps the corn plant standing upright.

The stalk also brings water and **nutrients** from the roots to other parts of the plant.

Corn stalks provide support

and nutrients to the rest of

the plant.

Corn Husks

The green leaves that grow around the corn are called the husk. The husk protects the corn from the weather and bugs.

Corn husks can be used for cooking things like **tamales**.

Corn Silk

Underneath the corn husk are thin strings called corn silk.

Corn silk is very important to the growth of corn. The silk catches pollen and brings it to the cob. Without silk, the corn kernels would not grow.

Corn silk is removed before corn is cooked. The strings can sometimes be hard to remove.

Corn Cobs

The corn cob is part of the flower of the corn plant. It is the hard core where the kernels grow.

Corn cobs are also called "ears" of corn.

Once the husk is pulled back,

corn cobs can be hung up to

dry.

Kernels

The kernels are the parts of the corn that we eat. They are also the seeds of the corn plant.

Kernels from some kinds of corn are dried and used to make popcorn.

There can be over 600 kernels

on a single cob of corn.

Life Cycle

First, a seed is planted in soil.

The seed grows into a sprout.

The sprout grows a hard stem

that is called a stalk.

The stalk then grows leaves

and a flower. The corn cob is

part of the flower.

Sprouts start out very small,

but the corn plant can grow

up to ten feet tall.

Where is Corn Grown?

Corn is grown on farms in large fields. It is not grown in the wild.

The United States **produces** more corn than any other country in the world. Most American corn is grown in a **region** called the corn belt.

Iowa, Illinois, Minnesota, and Nebraska are the top states for corn production in the United States.

Growing Corn

Corn is usually grown in long rows. The rows are spaced between two and three feet apart. This gives the plants room to grow.

Corn usually takes between sixty and one hundred days to be ready to harvest.

Corn is sometimes harvested by

hand.

A combine harvester is used on many farms to harvest the corn. It cuts the corn stalk and removes the cob from the stalk.

Then, it removes the kernels from the cob. The kernels are stored in the grain tank.

Combine harvesters make harvesting corn much easier than doing it by hand.

Transportation

Corn is transported in large **freight** trucks. If it is going to be sold in markets, it is transported on the cob.

Corn that is going to be used in other ways is usually taken off the cob first.

The unloader is part of the combine harvester. It loads the corn kernels into trucks for transportation.

Storage

Some corn is dried so that it can be stored for later use. It is stored in large buildings called grain bins.

The temperature inside the bin must be checked often. If the temperature isn't right, the corn inside can **spoil**.

People should never enter a

grain bin that is full. They can

be trapped under the corn.

Nutrition

Corn is a very healthy food.

It is full of vitamin B, vitamin

C, potassium, and fiber.

When eaten as popcorn,

corn is rich in **minerals** such

as zinc and magnesium.

Health Benefits

The **nutrients** in corn can help your body to stay healthy.

Potassium can help your heart to stay healthy. Fiber can help your body to get rid of waste.

The vitamins in corn can help

your eyes, brain, bones, and

teeth.

Corn as Food

Corn is a popular addition to many meals. The kernels can be removed and added to meals. It can also be eaten right off the cob.

Corn is believed to have been eaten at the first Thanksgiving.

It is also used to feed animals such

as cows, pigs, and chickens.

Other Uses for Corn

Corn has many uses other than food. It is also used to make things like soap, paint, and dyes.

Corn is also used to create a kind of fuel called biofuel. It can be used to power things like cars.

Biofuel may be better for the environment than some other fuels.

It produces less **carbon dioxide**.

Glossary

Carbon Dioxide: a gas that is found in the air

Freight: goods that are transported by truck, train, boat, or plane

Maize: another word for some kinds of corn

Minerals: substances that our bodies need to grow and work

Nutrients: something in food that helps people, animals, and plants grow

Produce: to make

Region: a large space or area

Spoil: to become rotten

Tamales: a Mexican food, meat and dough that are cooked in a corn husk

Victoria Blakemore is a first grade

teacher in Southwest Florida with a

passion for reading.

You can visit her at

www.elementaryexplorers.com

Also in This Series

Gray Wolves — Victoria Blakemore

Sloths — Victoria Blakemore

Flamingos — Victoria Blakemore

Camels — Victoria Blakemore

Koalas — Victoria Blakemore

Honey Bees — Victoria Blakemore

Pandas — Victoria Blakemore

Pangolins — Victoria Blakemore

White-Tailed Deer — Victoria Blakemore

Orcas — Victoria Blakemore

Giraffes — Victoria Blakemore

Corn — Victoria Blakemore

Meerkats — Victoria Blakemore

Echidnas — Victoria Blakemore

Walruses — Victoria Blakemore

Raccoons — Victoria Blakemore

Bald Eagles — Victoria Blakemore

Apples — Victoria Blakemore

Arctic Foxes — Victoria Blakemore

Red Pandas — Victoria Blakemore

Cassowaries — Victoria Blakemore

Tigers — Victoria Blakemore

Ladybugs — Victoria Blakemore

Moose — Victoria Blakemore

Beluga Whales — Victoria Blakemore

Leopards — Victoria Blakemore

Elephants — Victoria Blakemore

Jellyfish — Victoria Blakemore

Binturongs — Victoria Blakemore

Lions — Victoria Blakemore

Dolphins — Victoria Blakemore

Reindeer — Victoria Blakemore

Hammerhead Sharks — Victoria Blakemore

Hippos — Victoria Blakemore

Pumpkins — Victoria Blakemore

Peafowl — Victoria Blakemore

Chameleons — Victoria Blakemore

Florida Panthers — Victoria Blakemore

Aye-Ayes — Victoria Blakemore

Black Bears — Victoria Blakemore

Cheetahs — Victoria Blakemore

Manatees — Victoria Blakemore

Gingerbread — Victoria Blakemore

Polar Bears — Victoria Blakemore

Hot Chocolate — Victoria Blakemore

Orangutans — Victoria Blakemore

Coyotes — Victoria Blakemore

Marshmallows — Victoria Blakemore

Strawberries — Victoria Blakemore

Also in This Series

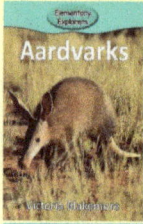

Aardvarks	Mako Sharks	Alligators	Frogs	Hedgehogs	Brown Bears	Bongos
Sea Turtles	Quokkas	Muskrats	Zebras	Red Foxes	Ring-Tailed Lemurs	Platypuses
Anteaters	Kangaroos	Rhinos	Jaguars	Wombats	Capybaras	Gorillas
Cats	Skunks	Butterflies	Dingoes	Snow Leopards	African Wild Dogs	Penguins
Whale Sharks	Wolverines	Warthogs	Caracals	Badgers	Seals	Hummingbirds
Pikas	Humpback Whales	Pumas	Lemonade	Llamas	Tulips	Ostriches
Sunflowers	Fennec Foxes	Sea Lions	Squirrels	Roses	Porcupines	Ice Cream